MODELLING SPE

ON TARGET

N°1

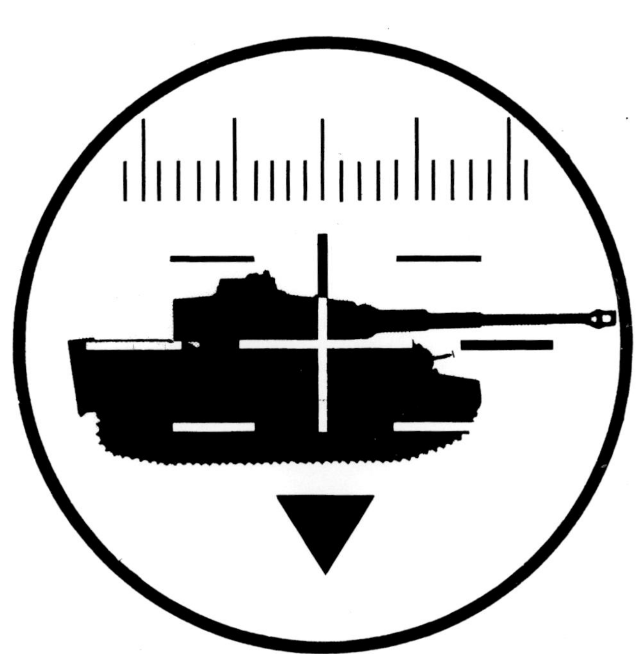

THE GERMAN TIGER TANKS

by François Verlinden

CONTENTS

Bibliography

- **Der Panzer-Kampfwagen Tiger und seine Abarten,**
  Walter J.Spielberger, Motorbuch Verlag
- **The Tiger Tanks**, Bryan Perrett, Osprey-Vanguard 20
- **Elefant and Maus (+ 100),**
  Walter J.Spielberger/John Milsom, AFV/Weapons Profile
- **PzKpfw VI Tiger I and Tiger II ('King Tiger'),**
  Peter Chamberlain/Chris Ellis, AFV/Weapons Profile

Published and distributed by   **The VLS Corporation**
811 Lone Star Drive
Lone Star Industrial Park
O'Fallon, MO 63366
USA

Project Manager & Chief Editor : François VERLINDEN

Text & Research :   François VERLINDEN

All scale modelling and model photography by François VERLINDEN

Printed in the USA.

Introduction

This book was originally conceived and published in 1984. Since that time, the hobby of armor modeling has undergone a tremendous resurgence. State of the art kits now abound from Tamiya, Dragon/DML, Italeri, and others. A decade ago I couldn't possibly imagine the number of armor accessories, updates, and figures that Verlinden Productions would eventually produce to fill a massive void in the hobby.

One of our first publishing priorities after moving VP from Belgium to the United States was to reprint this book. Along with "The Verlinden Way: Volume I" and "The System, Volume I: Figure Painting", this book has emerged as one of the best-selling hobby books of all time. Today's readers will immediately note that the kits and figures contained herein are of yesterday's technology, and some aren't even available any longer. Yet, it was my firm desire to maintain the integrity of the original text, reprinted in the American format, because what you are about to read is applicable even still - the art of accurately depicting a scale armor model.

By today's standards, the kits utilized in the creation of this book could be viewed by some as antiques. However, the techniques used to update and accurize these kits hold true. There have been only a handful of models ever manufactured that could be assessed as truly accurate straight from the box, which is one of the reasons Verlinden Productions was started in the first place. Thus, mastery of both basic and advanced detailing procedures remains a constant.

Another constant is the infatuation we armor modelers have with the German Tiger tank, a singular aspect of modeling which launched

this unique volume combining Tiger models with actual reference photos and information. The idea for this book spawned both the VP diorama and Showcase books as well as the Warmachines specials, and has earned the distinction of a classic manual. So, take a look at where we were 15 years back, and learn the advanced detailing tips that will help you create a scale masterpiece today.

The PzKpfw Tiger - A Short Development History

The best-known German heavy tank of World War II is generally refered to as the Tiger E, a designation it did not receive before 1944. When actual production began in 1942 it was officially known as PzKpfw VI Tiger Ausf.H (SdKfz 181). Between the two World Wars many countries were developing their tank arm. Amongst the former allies France was taking the lead with some magnificent designs, the US following closely, and Great Britain somewhat lagging behind. The Soviets weren't exactly sleeping either.

According to the Versailles Treaty Germany was not allowed to have tanks at all. When Hitler officially proclaimed that Germany would no longer live up to the treaty it was in a somewhat advantageous position. First of all the military and engineers had to start from scratch, thus not being prejudiced concerning tank design. Secondly of course, their designs were more up to date than those of their major future opponents. During the latter part of the 1930s the Allies were well aware of the existence of the PzKpfw I through IV, but only had a slight hunch as to the presence of the experimental heavies, the existence of which was masterfully contrived by Goebbel's propaganda service.

The early developments were outdated by 1937 so Henschel was asked to produce a new design. When this reached the prototype stage in the form of the DW2 (Durchbruchwagen 2) the Heereswaffenamt (army's armament department) had increased the requirement by specifying a more powerful gun. The contractors for this new design were Henschel, Porsche, MAN and Daimler-Benz. The design was however again abandoned at an early stage. Meanwhile Hitler, with his still unmatched insight into arms development, had specified a project: the 36t VK-3601. It called for heavy armor and and a high velocity gun in order to be able to deal with the heavily armored tanks like the French Char B and British Matilda, which, as experience had learned in the French campaign, were tough opponents. These specifications were again revised and resulted in the VK-4501 which called for the installation of the 88mm dual-purpose anti-aircraft / anti-tank gun and permitted an increase in weight to 45 tons. This was remarkable since the decision was made one month before the invasion of Russia and nobody yet knew of the qualities of the T-34.

By now Henschel and Porsche were the only contenders left in the race. The prototype s were to be ready by April 20, 1942, the birthday of the Führer. To meet this deadline Porsche and Henschel used the better features of the VK-3001 and VK-3601 designs. The trial took place at Rastenburg in time, the Henschel prototype being considered superior. This was to be the PzKpfwVI Tiger Ausf.H.

Production of the Tiger E continued for two years. In August 1944, when it ceased, 1,350 Tigers had been built. Records show that one vehicle was bought on behalf of the Imperial Japanese Army by Showa Tsusho Kaisha Ltd., but there is no evidence of it being delivered.

When the Tiger E had barely entered service it was already decided to produce an even better tank. All armor of the Tiger E was to the vertical and experience from Russia had learned that the sloping armour of the T-34 had far better ballistic properties. Germany wanted to get ahead of its opponents and use the extremely powerfull 88mm KwK 43/L71 in the new design. Again Henschel and Porsche were asked to submit prototypes for trial. Porsche submitted a modified design of his earlier entry with the turret at the rear, but a major drawback was the fact that the final drive of the tank was realised by means of electric motors which called for large supplies of copper, something Germany simply did not posses. Although Porsche was so confident he would win the contest that he started production of several dozen turrets, his design was rejected. Henschel's conventional lay-out was preferred and standarized as the PzKpfw VI Tiger Ausf.B (SdKfz 182), sometimes refered to as Tiger II, but generally known as the Königstiger (Royal Tiger to the Allies). The first fifty were equiped with the Porsche turrets, as they were readily available. The rounded front of the design was however considered dangerous as it could deflect shots down through the tin roof plate of the hull. The flat, backsloped front of the Henschel turret avoided this danger.

The most noticeable variant of the Tigers was the Sturmtiger based on the model B. A number of model Es were converted to Bergepanzer (recovery tanks). Some tanks of both models were modified as Panzerbefehlswagens (command tanks) by installing additional radios.

Panzerkampfwagen 'TIGER I' SdKfz 181 Ausführung E
(EARLY PRODUCTION TYPE)

Specifications

Total weight ------------------------------------:	56,900 kg
power plant ------------------------------------:	Maybach HL 210 P45V12 21 Liter 650PK
Armament ------------------------------------:	KWK 36 88mm L/56
	2 MG 34 one co-axial
Ammunition ------------------------------------:	92 rounds 88mm
	3,920 rounds 7.92 mm
Top speed ------------------------------------:	38 km/h
Crew ------------------------------------:	5

TIGER I in Tunisia

Tamiya's Tiger E is one of their early models, some fifteen years old. Considering this the quality is fairly good. General construction poses no problems as the fit is more than adequate. There is however a lack of sufficient exterior detail, the biggest problem being the absence of detail on the inside of the tracks. They are of the unrealistic, baggy type that many of the older Tamiya kits feature. It would not be a bad idea for Tamiya to make new tracks for this kit.

A final shortcoming is the fact that there are only two road-wheels per axle instead of three. One of these is wider than the other, thus simulating the two wheels that are bolted together. As these lay behind the single outer roadwheels the fault is not very obvious, so I did not bother to correct it.

This particular model was to become a very early type Tiger E which was only used in limited numbers in Tunisia. The very early types can be distinguished by the two pistol ports in the turret, the different shape of the hinged front mud-guards and the position of the headlights.

Ample detail is visible on this frontal view of the left side of a very early type Tiger E. On the later early production types the headlight was moved to the top of the hull roof-plate. Another typical feature of this type is the square grid mudguard that hinges on the rear. The mudguards on later types were double-hinged and extended farther over the tracks.

The cooling louvres have to be covered with wire mesh made from mosquito netting. The frames were made from plastic strip. The piping of the Feifel air filter system lacks flanges, and these were cut from plasticard. Note the small bolt heads on the towing cable clamps, engine cover and air filter cans. A scratch-built fire extinguisher has been added between the front right louvre and the towing cable.

The detailed front of both the turret hatches and the four gun travel lock mounting bolts.

A fine close-up of the lower right hand front of the hull. Note the gauge of the transmission bow guard and the shape of the backing plate with the five hex-head nuts. Also note the position of the lug for the shackle which differs from one production type to another.

The jack, toolbox, and jack mounts were detailed with plastic strip. The dents in the exhaust covers were made with a machining bit in a motor tool. Another hole in the bottom was filled with epoxy putty.

A rear quarter view of the finished turret showing another feature of the very early type Tiger : the second pistol port. Later extra port was taken from a second kit. Do not think it is a waste, because this secont kit is to become a late type Tiger which lacks pistol ports altogether. The ventilator cover hails from the Nichimo Tiger as this part is far better, detailed with strip and rod as was the toolbox. Note the heavy weld beads accomplished with the pyrograph.

The very early type features on my model have been realized by using plasticard, strip and rod. The mudguards were made from square grid plasticard. Note the tool clamps on the roof, the bolts and periscope on the radio operator's hatch and the butterfly nuts next to the ball mount, all made from plasticard, rod and strip. The rough weld beads were made with the pyrograph.

A detail shot of the front and underside of the hull. The transmission bow guard was made thicker by adding a piece of 1.5mm heavy plasticard. The backing plate and nuts were made from 0.8mm plasticard. Note the holes in the bottom of the hull, which serve to mount the electric motor and switch for the model, have been filled with epoxy putty. The two roadwheels on each axle are clearly visible. The wider inner wheels, which simulate the two bolted together, are hardly visible when the tracks are installed.

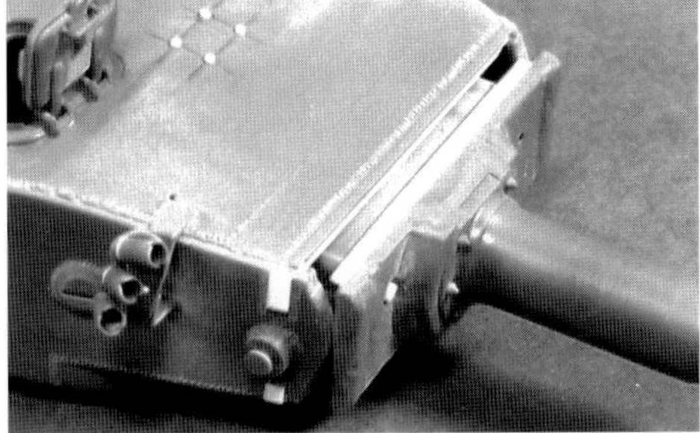

A detail shot of the right side of the turret showing the detailed smoke grenade launchers, the heavy weld beads and the interlocking front plates added from plasticard.

Above : A close-up of the desert water hole. The water effect was accomplished by painting the relevant area of the base plate with various shades of green and yellow. Subsequently the whole was covered with a heavy coat of gloss varnish.

At Left : The dromedary and Bedouin figures are from Heller. The upper part of the figure is that of the lieutenant, the lower part is from the Bedouin. The basket and water pouches hanging from the saddle are from Historex. Note the realistic desert soil: the embedded rocks, the tumble weed and the cactus. Remember that 80% of the world's deserts consist of rock, not sand.

A frontal view from above. The tank crew was composed with figures from various kits. The realistic pose was achieved by using spare arms and heads. Note the heavy metal sheen on those parts of the tracks that come in direct contact with the ground.

The finished Tiger E of S.Pz.Abt.501 on the desert diorama. Rudimentary camouflage netting has been applied on the hull sponsons. Personal equipment was attached to the rear of the turret. Note the heavy weathering of the rear part of the hull and the realistic looking tubing of the air filter. Be careful when weathering-tanks in a desert scene barely show any rust but do feature a lot of worn of paint.

This picture reveals all important details on the rear end of the engine compartment cover. The dome in the top left corner covers the telescopic air intake pipe for deep water wading.

Ample detail on this photo of the left rear end with the track toolbox mount, partially hinged mud guard, shackle lug and dome cover of the draw bolt to adjust the track tension.

A good picture of the Feifel air filter cans from the rear.

Here the forward side of the cans are visible. Note the way they are mounted.

To the left :
As you can see on this picture the smoke grenade ejectors on most kits can do with some extra detail.

To the right :
The forward side of the smoke grenade ejectors. Note the way they are mounted.

Detail on this photo includes the clamps for the gun cleaning road and towing cable.

This shot from above clearly shows the shape of the radio operator's hatch with the periscope cover.

A close-up of the machinegun ball mount in the hull. The large hole is for the gun, the small hole takes the sighting telescope. The threaded studs with the butterfly nuts serve to mount a dust cover.

The top of the commander's cupola with the spring-loaded hatch. The two small tubes serve to mount additional distance measuring equipment.

A detail shot of the loader's hatch. Opening of the heavy cover is assisted by means of a spring loaded push-rod mounted on the inside of the roof.

A close-up of the pistol port, on the left side of the turret. The awkward position behind the commander's seat made extensive use of the port doubtful. For this reason it was deleted on the late type turrets.

This picture shows you the thickness of the armor, the rough texture, the still neat welds and the gun trunions all in once.

The exact shape of the center section of the gun mantlet is clearly depicted here. The serial number is a simple weld bead. Obviously some small arms fire has eaten some chunks out of the barrel sleeve.

Panzerkampfwagen 'TIGER I' SdKfz 181 Ausführung E
(LATE PRODUCTION TYPE)

Specifications

Total weight	56,900 kg
power plant	Maybach HL 210 P45V12 24 Liter 700PK
Armament	KWK 36 88mm L/56
	2 MG 34 one co-axial
Ammunition	92 rounds 88mm
	3,920 rounds 7.92 mm
Top speed	38 km/h
Crew	5

The Workshop

This repair shop shadow box project involved extensive converting and detailing of the Tamiya Tiger model, a load of scratch-building, an intensive search for accessories, figures, the making of printed circuits and so on and so forth. All in all it was a tremendous job but the final result is worth the trouble. First of all this Tiger was to be one of the final production types. As the Tamiya kit is an early production type this means that apart from minor detail differences, the turret had to be changed as well as the running gear. The late production type turret did not have a pistol port. To reduce cost the commander's cupolas were taken from the Tamiya Panther. Another cost and raw material reducing measure was deleting the rubber lined roadwheels and fitting steel-lined roadwheels instead. In concrete this means that the pistol port has to be closed up, the cupola has to be removed and replaced by the cupola from the Nichimo Tiger. This goes for the roadwheels as well. Why not use the Nichimo Tiger then? Simply because it is too much out of proportion. It is much better to take the Tamiya Tiger and convert it by cannibalizing a Nichimo kit. In respect of cost you will about break even. Timewise you will save a lot.

To prepare the model for this scene a lot of extras had to be scratch-built. An opened engine compartment is no good without an engine. The compartment itself had to be detailed and some detail in the fighting compartment did not seem a bad idea either.

Then, of course, the exterior had to be reworked. To represent the action a few figures had to be converted to suit the desired poses. Much of the typical repair shop gear, like the welding transformer, the workbench and closet had to be scratch-built. Other accessories, like hammers, wrenches, compressor and so on were either taken from the Italeri Field Tool Shop or the Tamiya Tool Set on 1/20 scale. Much of the work involved was consumed by casting the garage walls and making the shadow box. The interior wall is made out of five sections of three different types. To obtain the life-like effect, masters of these different types were made of very fine styrofoam. This takes some time and quite a lot of experience. Next in line were the female molds in RTV rubber.

Finally the wall sections in epoxy plaster were cast in these moulds. Painting and weathering them is again a matter of experience, but for those who want to take a crack at it, the basics are explained in the Verlinden Productions catalogue / handbook. The next pages will give an illustrated step-by-step description of the most important stages of this project.

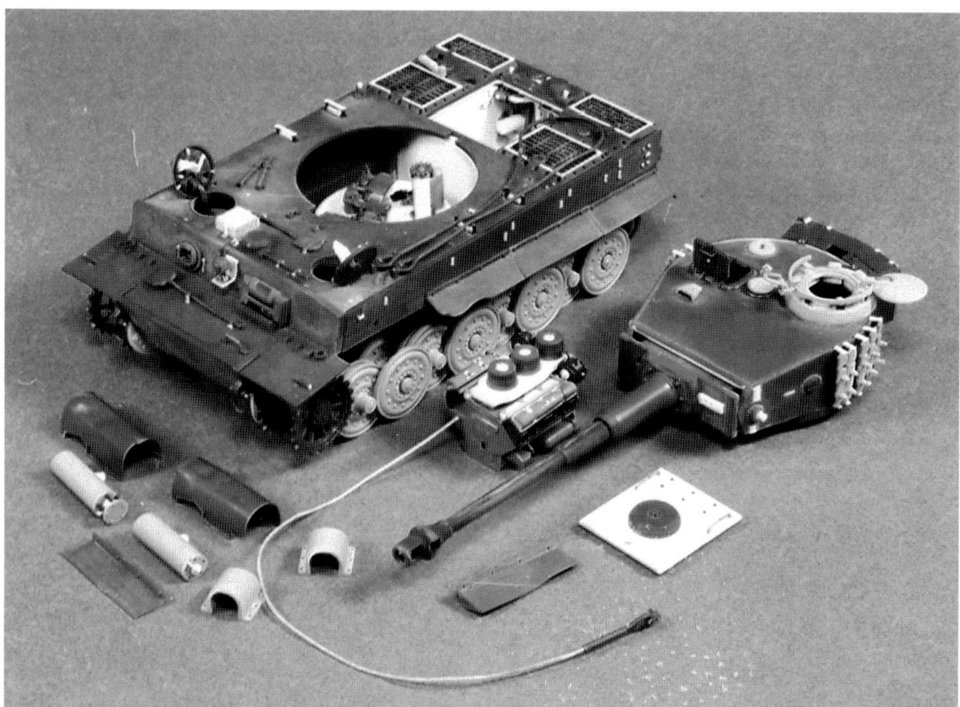

The complete array of scratch-built and converted parts for this super-detailed Tiger I. Most of the home-made parts are in white plasticard. It would be wise for you to examine this picture closely. Do not let it discourage you. First of all, you do not have to go for all of it at once and secondly, it is not as tough as it may seem.

To get something that closely resembles a Maybach engine I had to wander through all of my scrapboxes, but still a lot had to be custom made.

To adapt the steel lined roadwheels from the Nichimo kit to the Tamiya hull, the shafts of the latter had to be cut off and holes drilled to accomodate the shafts that come with the Nichimo wheels.

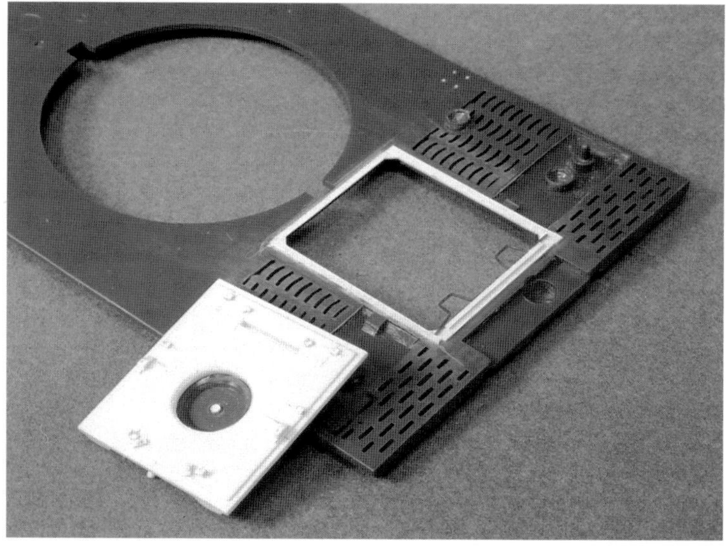

An opened engine compartment cover calls for a detailed inside of same. This picture shows the inside of the scratch-built hatch plus the sills on which it rests when closed.

A lot of cutting and drilling was involved to get this result, but finally the new roadwheels are in place.

The outside of the finished engine compartment hatch. The only original part left is the breather cover. The rest was carefully scratch-built.

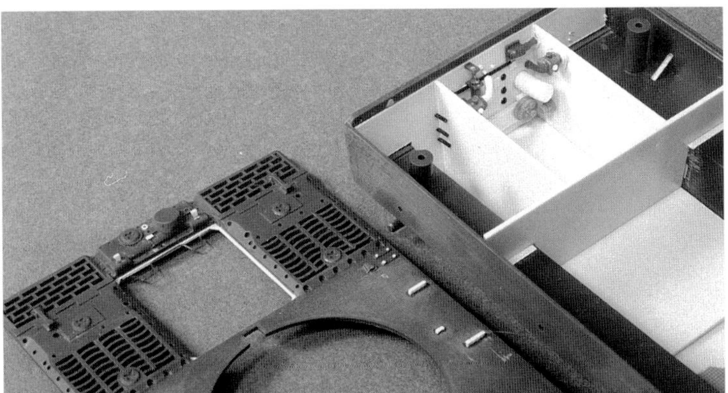

This picture gives a fair idea of the work involved to create a somewhat life-like engine compartment. You can rest assured that quite a lot of research is involved.

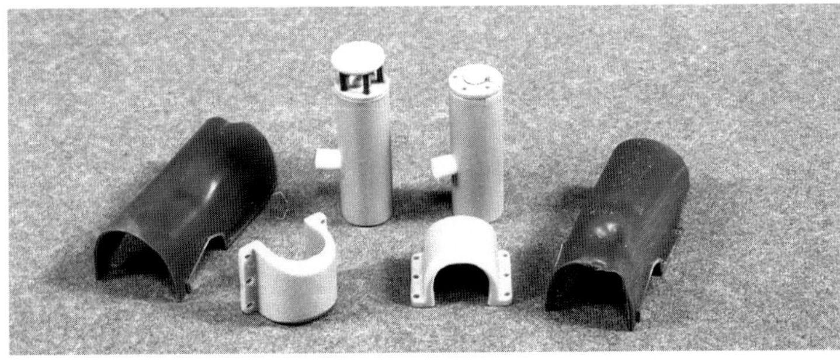

Above we see the separate exhausts from Nichimo and the covers from Tamiya.

The top picture shows the reworked rear end of the model. Below we see a picture of the rear hull plate that corresponds with the picture above. It was a matter of look-and-do.

The conversion work on the turret has started. The cupola has been replaced, the turret ventilator is moved to the center of the roof, a loader's periscope is fitted and the sighting telescope holes in the gun mantlet have been reinforced with plastic strip.

The turret interior was detailed using many pictures as reference. It may very well be that some of this detail is no longer visible, but you can never be sure about that beforehand and it's tough to add detail when the model is finished.

The engine is test fitted in the compartment. Scratch-building into the blue is no good. Test fitting is a part of detail-modelling that is not to be underestimated.

A picture of the finished, unpainted turret. Note the small added detail like the mounting strips for the spare track links, the locks on the stowage bins, etc.

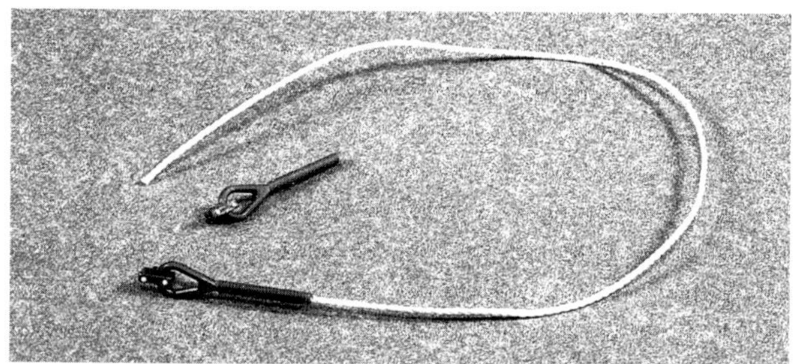

The only realistic towing cable is a flexible towing cable. Good rope as used by ship modellers is very well suited.

Some more proof of the necessary research is obvious on this picture. To complete the front interior a search for good pictures in several books is a must.

Some of the exterior detail changes are obvious on this picture. The head-light had to be repositioned, the driver's and radio-operator's hatches needed more detail on the inside and the late type turret was also in need of small additional detail.

A detail shot of the final type front fender. Note the basic difference compared to the early type fenders. The shield is non-standard.

Close-up of the drive sprocket and late type roadwheels. Note the height of the track links and compare this to the Tamiya tracks.

Italeri's Field Tool Shop is a good source for equipment needed in scenes like this.

Some plasticard, spare wheels and a race car steering-wheel make up this home made welding transformer.

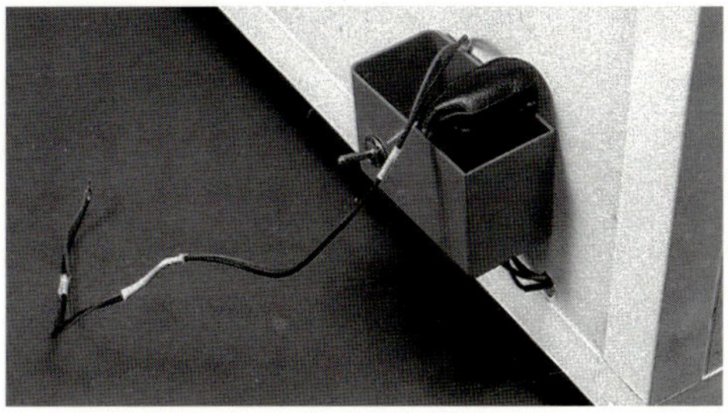

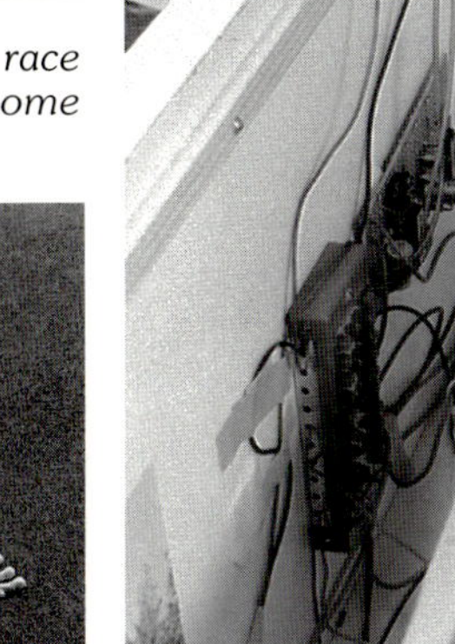

The main power switch on the back of the shadow box.

The finished, unpainted scratch-built work-bench and locker. A good stock of various gauges of plasticard is an absolute must for the scratch-builder.

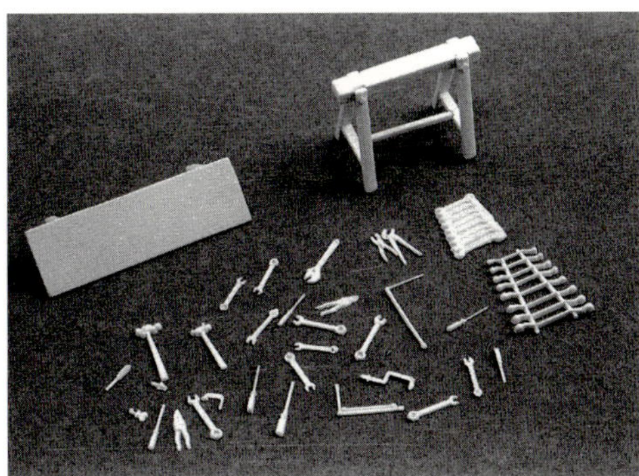

Some more scratch-built repair shop items plus an array of tools that were carefully sanded off the back of the tool-box of the Tamiya 1/20 scale race track set.

A view of the electrical wiring and printed circuits on the inside of the shadow box. The printed circuits to obtain a realistic arc and the typical sound of the welding gear can either be bought as pre-fab parts or can be home made using the widely available instructions.

An overall view of the shadow box interior. By the time you have reached this stage, you have come a long way. For instance, it takes a lot of time to figure out how, when and where the electronic gimmicks have to go. You need a suitable background picture to place behind the windows. The most favorable position of the model, figures and accessories has to be determined and so on.

A cozy corner of the shadow box. The stove from Galia metal castings has come to life by means of a LED. The coal box is scratch-built; model railroad coal is used to fill it up. Shovel, bucket, etc. came from the scrap-box.

Do not think this is a waste of accessories. Only half of it is real. The rest is reflected in the mirror that forms the right wall of the repair shop.

The finished workbench. By carefully looking at this picture you can determine for yourself what small detail makes this little scene so life-like.

This picture does not really need any comment. It will tell enough by just looking at it. When starting on a diorama like this, just ask to take a look in a nearby garage to get in the right mood.

Another example of how carefully selected and placed accessories can add to realism.

To the right : This tool rack was scratch-built from rod and plasticard. Tools from various sources, a good paint job and some imagination make it look very realistic.

By carefully selecting the frame through which you look, you can draw the viewer's attention to a certain first impression which is important. A second look will reveal the small details.

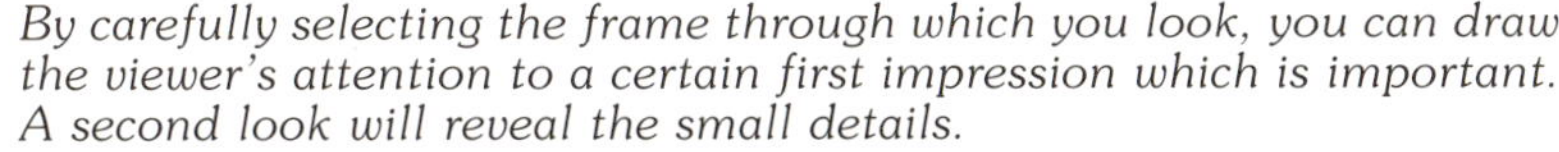

Shadow box dimensions / Scratch built accessories

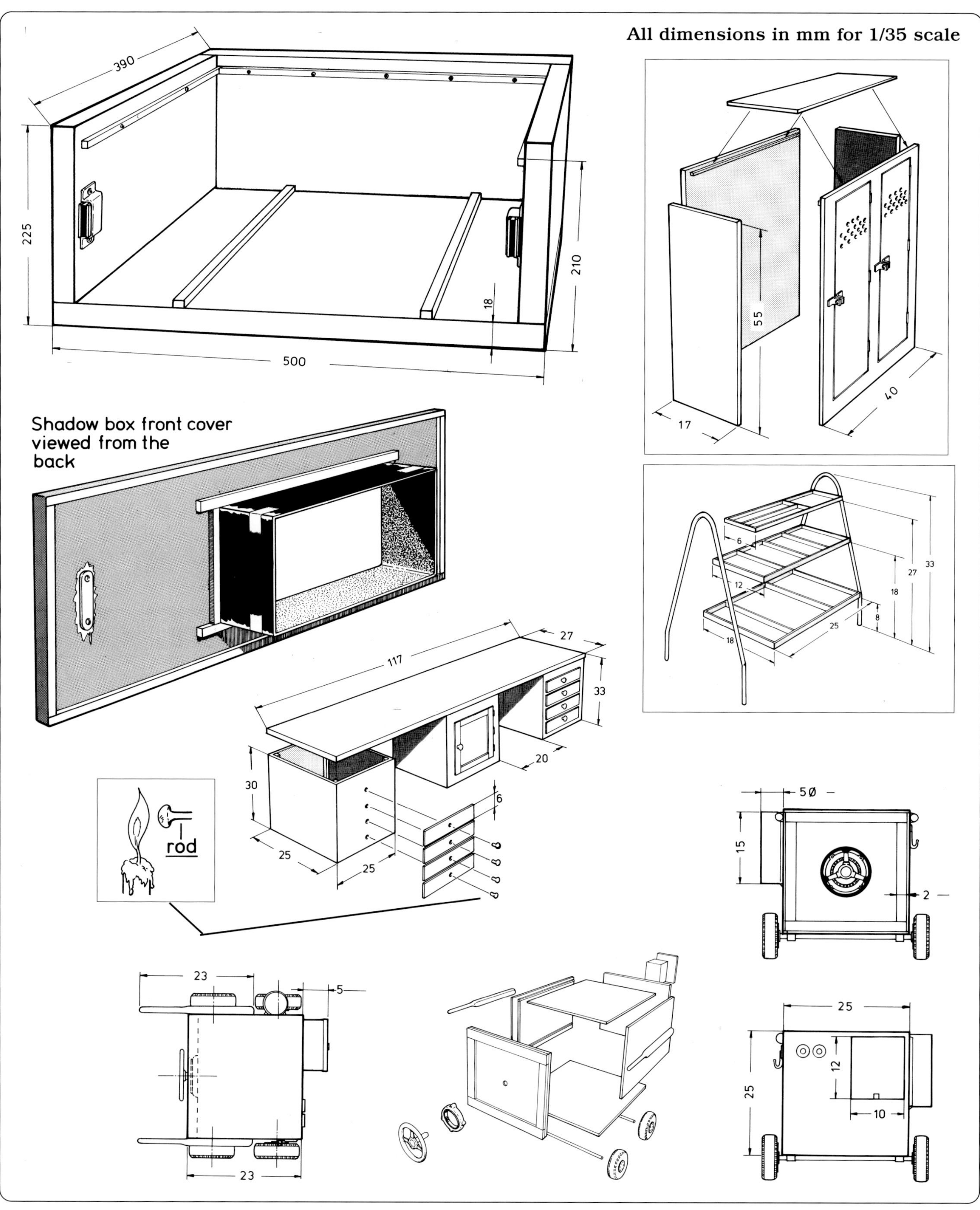

TIGER I Interior

An overall view of the driver's compartment. Normal steering was effected by means of the wheel. For on-the-spot turning the large levers astride the seat wre used. In the center is the vision block. The wheel in the lower right corner of same serves to open and close the slit on the outside. In the top left corner of the picture is the direction indicator i.e. a compass.

Good picture of the radio operator's compartment are rare. At left is the mounting rack for the radio sets on top of the gearbox. In the left foreground is the actuating handle of the bilge pump. The gunner needs both hands to guide the ammunition belt and fire the gun. For this reason the gun-mount features a headpad to facilitate aiming of the breech-heavy gun. In the right foreground is the adjustable back-lean.

A detail shot of the instrument panel on top of the gearbox. Above it are two spare vision blocks. Mounted on the gearbox is the gear pre-selector lever.

The sponson area in the radio operator's compartment is used to stock machinegun ammo, gun spare parts and tools and a first-aid kit. The clamps on the hull side-plate mounted a spare vision block and a gas-mask container.

The left side turret interior. The commander's seat has the turret rotating mechanism directly in front of it. Barely visible behind the seat is the pistol port. Further detail includes several clamps for gas-mask containers, signal pistol, etc.and intercom panel.

Interior detail of turret's rear. At the extreme left is the opened escape hatch. Next to it is the main power distributor box with the turret ventilator immediately above. In the center are several containers for the headsets, spare vision blocks and signal pistol cartridges. At the right is the commander's seat with the back-lean in raised position which thus serves as seat or stand when the commander's hatch is open.

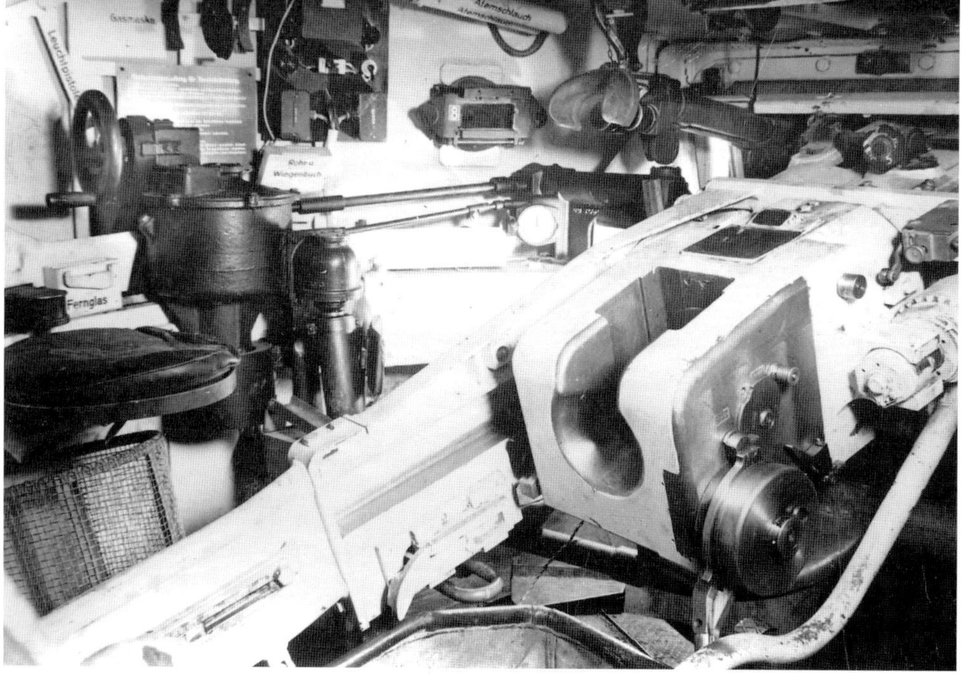

An overall view looking at the forward left corner. Detail on the gun breech is clearly visible. Above the breech is the gunner's sighting telescope. This picture also offers a view on the turret rotating mechanism. Fast rotation is effected through activating the hydraulic mechanism on the turret floor. Fine adjustments are made by turning the handwheel in front of the gunner. In emergency situations the commander can assist the gunner by rotating the small handwheel on top of the traversing gear casing. General color of the Tiger interior is light buff with black detail.

A good view of the entire right side of the breech. The canvas bag catches the ejected shell cases. On the right side of the breech is one of the two recoil dampers with the co-axial machine-gun next to it. The loader faces towards the rear of the turret.

The gun elevating mechanism is positioned under the breech, slightly to the right of it. In the top left corner beneath the sighting telescope is the horizontally positioned turret rotating hand-wheel.

This picture clearly depicts the hydraulic turret drive unit. In the center of the photo is the pedal unit which actuates the drive mechanism. The small pedal is hooked up to the coaxial machinegun. In the lower right corner is the fire extinguisher. Note that the gunner's seat is attached to the gun elevating system. The gunner's position in the Tiger was quite uncomfortable.

The right side of the turret interior. On the right is the closed escape hatch, in the center some ammo bags for the coaxial machinegun. The large black pipe is a hydraulic cylinder which serves as counter-balance for the barrel-heavy main gun.

A detail shot of the ammo stowage bins in the hull sponsons. Six bins hold a total of 92 rounds.

A view into the empty engine compartment. Forward is to the left. Three torsion bars are visible on the bottom. Two of the four fuel tanks are positioned to the left and the right of the engine in the lower part of the compartment, under the cooling radiator compartments. The two other tanks are in the forward section of the latter.

Panzerkampfwagen 'TIGER II' SdKfz 182 Ausführung B
(HENSCHEL TURRET)

Total weight	68,000 kg
power plant	Maybach HL 230 P30V12 24 Liter 700PK
Armament	KWK 43 88mm L/71
	2 MG 34 one co-axial
Ammunition	84 rounds 88mm
	5,850 rounds 7.92 mm
Top speed	41,5 km/h
Crew	5

Defense of the 'REICH'

The Nichimo kit of the Königstiger has been around for quite some time. It is very worthwhile making as the detail is very crisp and quite sufficient. Just a little extra-detailing makes this kit into a very impressive model.

The scene on this diorama is typical for the final days of the Third Reich. The Germans were going through a last effort to try and stem the Allied onslaught that was crushing their "Heimland" from all sides. This often resulted in fierce street fighting which took a necessary high toll of men and material. At that time the heavy tank units were at the disposal of the territorial commanders and were sent from one scene to another wherever the pressure was heaviest. As history tells us it was all in vain. The set-up of the diorama is almost classical and is a very good example to learn the basics of diorama composition. When examining the scene you will soon realise that it tells some sort of story on its own. This is vital for every diorama. The figures have to be related to each other. Note that they are all facing the same direction while some of them are engaged in a conversation. The secondary vehicle in the scene is there to fill the yard, but it does not look as if it was placed there with that purpose in mind. Somehow the man with the wounded arm is closely related to it. The array of accessories brings life into the scene but also serves to fill empty spots.

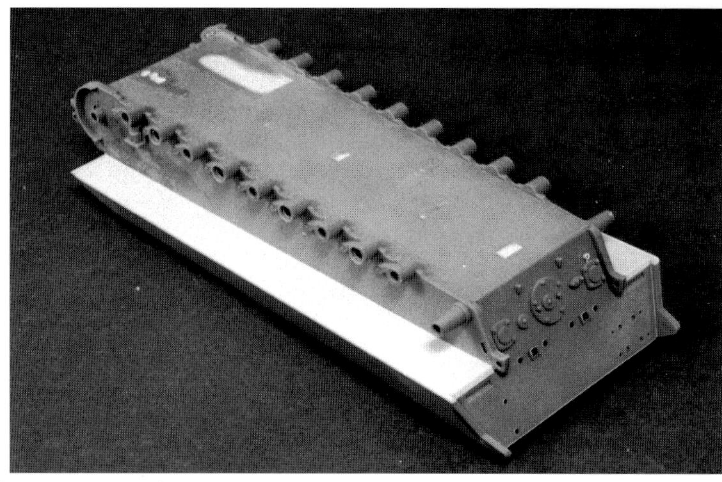

The kit's hull sponsons are open on the underside. As it is a rather awkward sight to see the tracks when looking through the hatches, so these have to be blanked off with plasticard. This goes for the holes in the bottom that serve to mount the motorization parts as well.

The kit is very well detailed. Just a few tool clamps and track skirt mounting strips from plasticard had to be added. Note the weld beads made with the pyrograph.

A general view of the finished, unpainted front section. Even at this distance the rough tooled armor plates are very clear.

A close-up of the hull front. The Tigers have interlocking armor plates that can be simulated by cutting and machining the locks. Again note the weld beads and roughened texture.

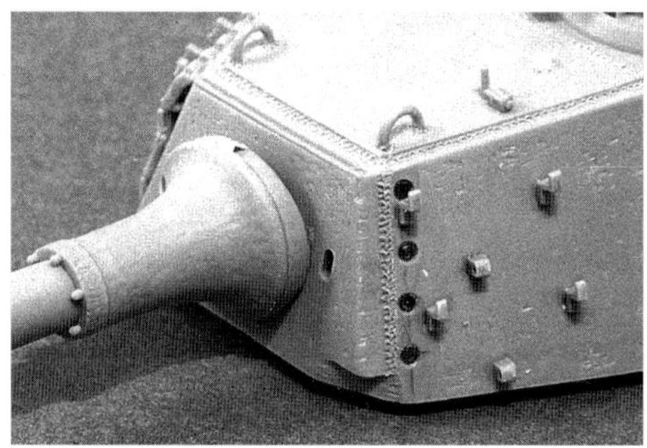

The turret armor plates can also do with a treatment. In general all armor plating on model tanks is way too smooth, except for the latest Tamiya kits. When armour plates are rolled a fair amount of slag remains after the material has cooled down. When this slag is removed in view of further processing the plates show the typical rough texture that looks like slate. The four holes in the side are later plugged with pieces of rod. On the real tank these serve to line up the front plate during construction.

In this picture the effect of the rough plate is perfectly clear. To achieve this effect a small ball shaped drill bit is put in the motor tool. With the latter at a low rev setting you carefully touch the plastic at random and in different directions. Do not push too hard or the plastic will melt.

As is obvious from this picture the rear of the hull can also do with a little extra-detailing. Some pieces of strip make up clamps for the jack, toolbox, towing hooks, etc.

The only important lacking feature of this kit is the wire mesh on the cooling louvres. These were made from mosquito netting. The framework around the front louvres was of course made from plasticard.

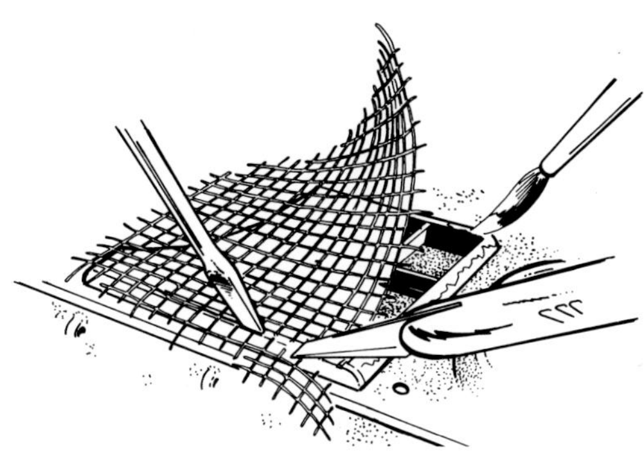

To fix the wire mesh you should apply a fair amount of glue to soften the plastic and push the netting in firmly. This can be trimmed to size when the glue has set.

The fences are all made from balsa strip and square rod. When the parts are glued together the whole is washed with a dark brown mixture and then drybrushed. The posters come from various sources including our VP accessories range.

The MDA house ruin is finished and the first layout of the diorama is made on the base plate. The cobblestone street is printed relief carton from Faller. Note that the general line of the diorama is not perpendicular to any side of the base plate as this would give a very dull, unrealistic apperance.

Of course a house has a detailed interior as well. The bare brick parts are simulated with printed relief carton from Faller cut to size. The plaster is simulated with off-white carton which, when cut to shape, is glued to the brick carton. Seen here are the parts for the ground floor and first floor facades.

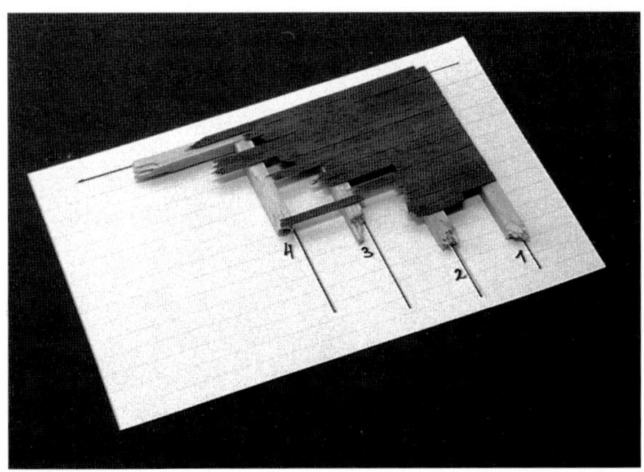

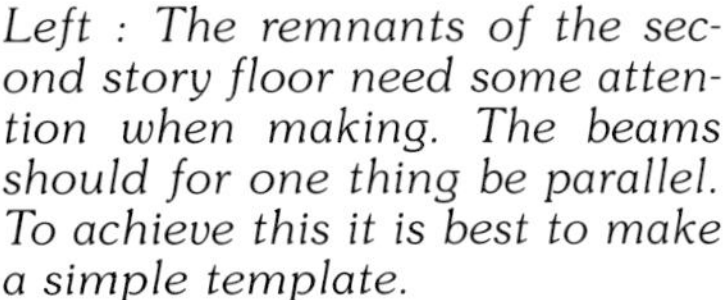

Right : The ground floor interior facade ready for installation. It takes some care to make the various parts match up with the ruin.

Left : The remnants of the second story floor need some attention when making. The beams should for one thing be parallel. To achieve this it is best to make a simple template.

A realistic effect on a diorama featuring a ruined house requires a lot of rubble, broken roof tiles, etc. All of this is readily available from well-stocked hobby shops.

The finished interior of the ruin. Traces of fire have been liberally applied by using the drybrush and wash techniques. Note the lighter spots on the side wall which indicate that there must have been some pictures hanging there at one time.

As secondary vehicle on my diorama I chose to use the Kübelwagen from Italeri. Note the traces of fire on the side wall of the ruin. The electrical wire mount on the ruin is from Italeri. The bare bush in the foreground is a root from my back yard.

A view from above of what used to be the neighboring house. Note the large pile of debris. This can never be enough. Looking at real pictures will give you a fair idea of what it should look like.

Note the small details like the street name plate, the antique lamp post, ammo crates, etc. These were either scratchbuilt, acquired through a hobby shop that carries model rail road accessories, or taken from the VP accessories range.

A close-up of the top of the lamp post. The glass is a broken piece from a slide frame.

A fine study of the tank crew. Their natural pose was achieved by trying out several combinations of figure parts. It is wise to always keep any surplus arms, legs and so on in seperate boxes for future projects. The so-called scrap-box is the modeler's greatest treasure.

KING TIGER Details

A fine study of the hull front plate showing the rough texture to advantage.

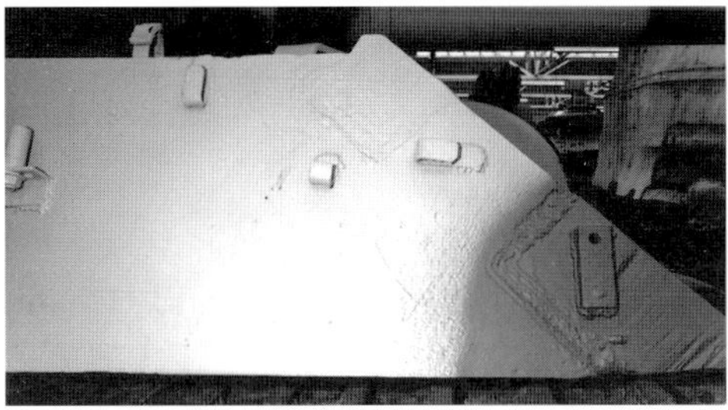

A close-up of the interlocking hull front and side plates. Note the thickness of the front plate and the rough finish of the weld.

A detail study of the right rear showing the gauge of the hull side plates, the cover of the track tension draw-bolt and the pattern of the track links.

One of the many styles of registration. Type of lettering could even vary within a unit. Good documentation is imperative when modeling a particular tank.

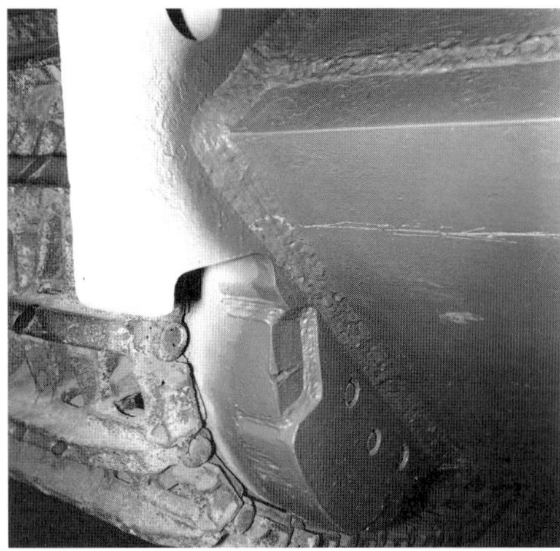

The interlocking plates that make up the final drive housing. The various parts did not always fit too well, the reason being that most tanks were built by so-called 'volunteers' from occupied countries and they, of course, did not care too much about clean fits and crisp finish.

This picture clearly shows the details of the Henschel turret featuring the flat face plate and the typical gun mantlet. The latter is a one piece casting as is obvious from the longitudinal seam. This was the final production version of the Tiger B.

Above : An overall view of the Königstiger preserved at Laglaise/Belgium.
Right : A general view of the left side showing clamps and mounting strips for towing cables, gun cleaning rods, track skirts, etc.

Jagdpanzer VI Panzerjäger TIGER Ausführung B SdKfz 186

Specifications

Total weight	70,000 kg
Power plant	Maybach HL 230 P30V12 24 Liter 700PK
Armament	12.8 cm Pak 80 L/55
	1 MG 34
	1 MG 42
Ammunition	38 rounds 12.8 cm
Top speed	38 km/h
Crew	6

Defense Position

To make this model I chose to use the Nichimo kit as the Tamiya kit is less accurate. Not that the Nichimo model is perfect, but the basic shapes are good apart from the so-called 'Saukopfblende' or sow-head mantlet which is undersized. Further extra-detailing is however a piece of cake.

While Henschel was still tooling up for the Tiger B production, the Heereswaffenamt ordered development of an assault gun based on the Tiger B. It was to be equipped with the Krupp 12.8 cm gun in a fixed superstructure. The wooden mock-up was presented to Hitler in October 1943, the first production type being delivered in April 1944. With its 75 tons this armored vehicle was the heaviest ever produced in this era.

As from March 1945 the availability of the 12.8cm gun was rather poor. Hitler ordered the round up of every gun wherever it might be. To overcome the temporary shortage it was ordered to equip up to a maximum of 50 Jagdtigers with the 8.8cm Pak 43/3 (Sf) (Sd.Kfz 185), constructed by Steyr-Daimler-Puch A.G.. The total number of Jagdtigers produced till the end of the war amounted to 70. Ten experimental Jagdtigers were fitted with an easier to produce Porsche suspension. Trials were satisfying but the course of the war made further development impossible.

Only a second look tells you that this is a photo of a model. For plastic model photography one needs a good camera and background material but the results often make the investment worthwhile.

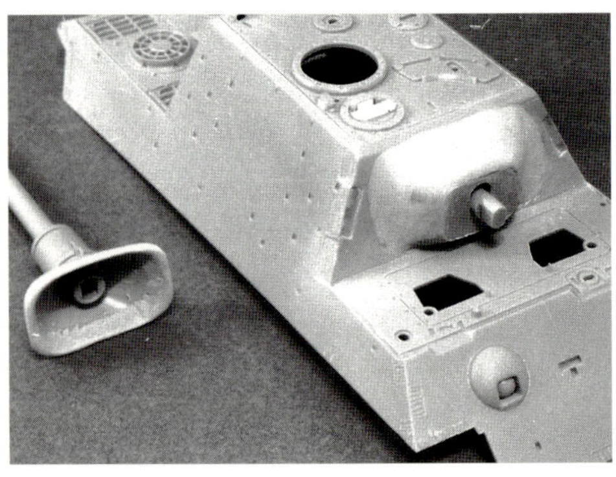

The main shortcomings of the Nichimo kit are the undersized superstructure front plate casting and the corresponding gun mantlet, but this is easy to overcome by using epoxy putty.

Apart from the small details on the sides, some extra detail has to be added around the driver's and radio operator's hatches as well.

At right : Planning the initial layout of a diorama calls for some care. Several combinations are tried before the final composition is decided upon.

In general track skirts did not seem to have a great affinity with the parent tank. Many of them were lost in the early stages of operational life. Leaving these skirts off of your model means you have to provide mounting strips.

This photo clearly depicts the interlocking armor plates and the array of weld beads on the rear super-structure of the Jagdtiger.

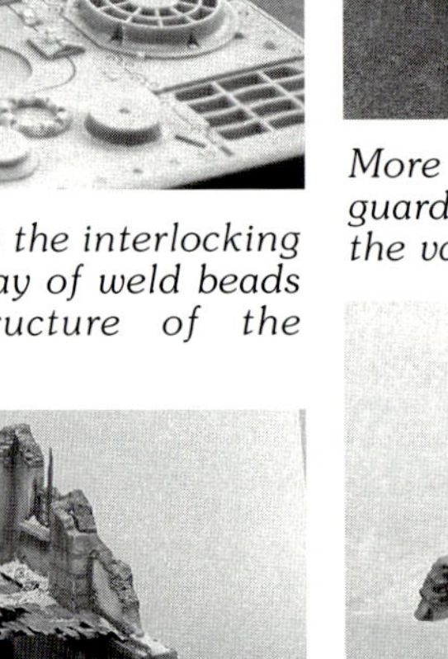

It is still a long way from the trial layout as seen above to this final result. Making a ruined house calls for a lot more than just glueing a handful of rubble to the base plate. The various items have to 'fit' into the scene but should not vanish into the whole.

This picture offers an overall view of the extra-detailed right side. Apart from the skirt mounting strips the added detail includes tool and towing cable clamps.

More detail includes the hinged mudguards and some plastic strip to simulate the various clamps on the hull rear plate.

This MDA kit of a ruined interior serves as a realistic setting for the Jagdtiger.

Painting and finishing MDA kits is explained in the Verlinden Productions catalogue/handbook. This picture is to give you an idea of what you may do to detail them.

Above : The massive silhouette of the Jagdtiger stands out nicely against the background of the ruined interior. This picture again illustrates the importance of ample consideration while composing a diorama. The highest item is in the back, the lowest is in front. And ...... the scene tells the story of a Jagdtiger backing into hideout under guidance of the radio operator.

Let us take a closer look at a tank crew member. Here you should note the authentic headset with the wiring, and the shading of the uniform.

It may be useful to say a word or two on jerrycans. There is a definite difference between the German and the US type. The ones seen here are of the German type. Compare them to the US type. You may mix the two types on scenes from the final stages of WWII as both sides captured large fuel supplies.

HUNTING TIGER Details

Close-up of the commander's periscope. The nature of the small hatch is not altogether clear. It may very well have accomodated an additional sighting periscope.

The commander's hatch in detail. Directly in front of it is the periscope as seen on the left picture. In the top left corner a small part of the kidney shaped hatch for the gunner's sighting periscope can be made out.

An overall view of the hull roof plate with the driver's hatch and the radio operator's hatch. Note the shape of the driver's periscope cover and the electrical lead for the single headlamp.

At right :The exact shape of the cast superstructure front plate is very obvious here. Note the rough texture of the plate and the gun mantlet.

A detail shot of the double escape hatch on the rear of the superstructure. Small details were different from one Jagdtiger to the other depending on where it was constructed.

The interlocking superstructure plates.

The radio operator's hatch with the hull ventilator dome in the top right corner.

An overall view of the left side of the Jagdtiger preserved in the RAC Museum at Bovington Camp. Note the array of hooks and clamps and the remainders of the Zimmerit anti-magnetic mine paste.

This picture clearly depicts the shape of the 'Saukopfblende' or sow-head mantlet.

This view of the left hand front offers a good impression of the general shape of the Jagdtiger and the remainders of the zimmerit.

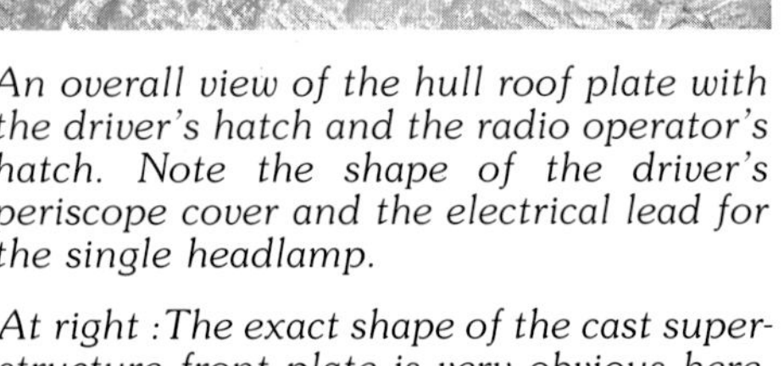

Detail on this picture includes the exhaust system, mud guards, lifting and towing lugs and tool clamps.

Panzerkampfwagen 'TIGER II' SdKfz 182 Ausführung B
(PORSCHE TURRET)

Specifications

Total weight	-------------------------------------:	68,000 kg
Power plant	-------------------------------------:	Maybach HL 230 P30V12 24 Liter 700PK
Armament	-------------------------------------:	KWK 43 88mm L/71
		2 MG 34 one co-axial
Ammunition	-------------------------------------:	84 rounds 88 mm
		5,850 rounds 7.92 mm
Top speed	-------------------------------------:	41,5 km/h
Crew	-------------------------------------:	5

Supply Point

A supply stop is one of those friendly scenes that offer you the possibility to use quite a few accessories. There is always room for a lot of ammunition, fuel drums and jerrycans, rations, etc. Of course, this means that you have to assemble the lot, but the result is worthwhile. The Königstiger on this diorama is of the early type with one of the fifty Porsche turrets.

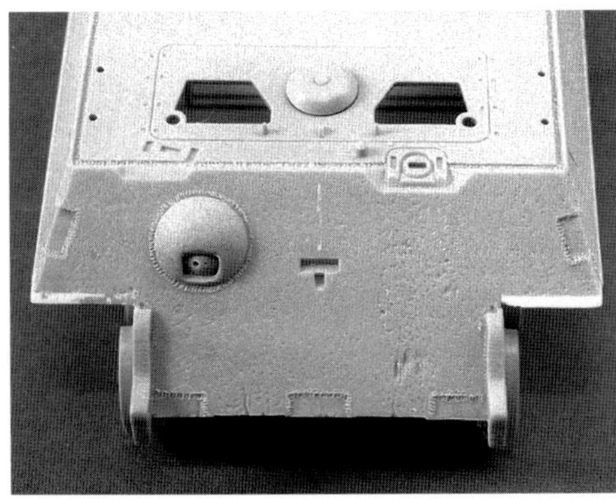

The finished unpainted front of the model. Note the rough texture and the sculpted interlocks with the weld beads.

Two important missing features have been added. First of all the typical intake and then the cover plates over the cooling air intakes and the radiator compartment to keep Molotov cocktails out. Then, a fire extinguisher had to be added.

The outer part of the mudguards was hinged. As this part had to be folded back I chose to make a new one.

The rear of the hull without the exhausts and the mounts for toolbox, spare track links, jack, etc..

Apart from some small detail and, of course, the rough texture and weld beads the turret can be built straight from the box.

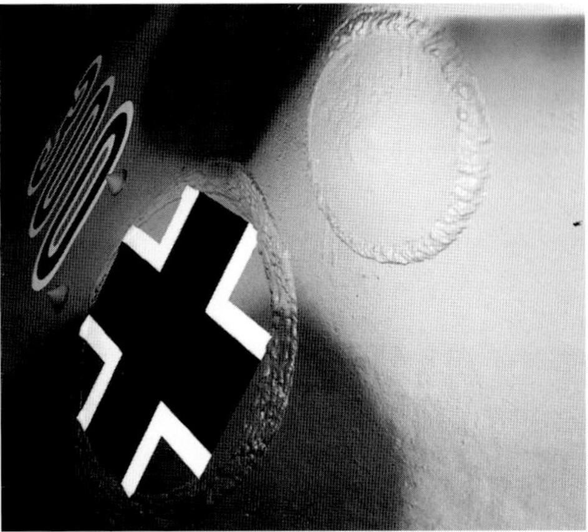

The original turret design obviously provided for a vision slit and/or pistol port on the commander's side. These holes were plugged. Do not forget to add this on your model.

Because I planned to leave off the left rear mud guard I had to add the mounting strips.

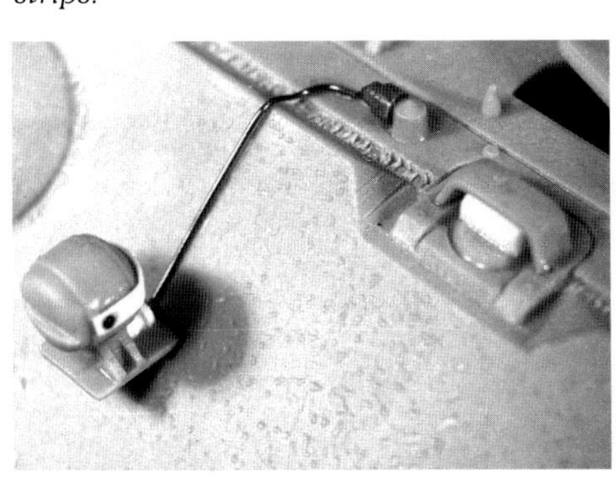

The single headlight can do with some additional detail and, of course, the often forgotten electrical lead.

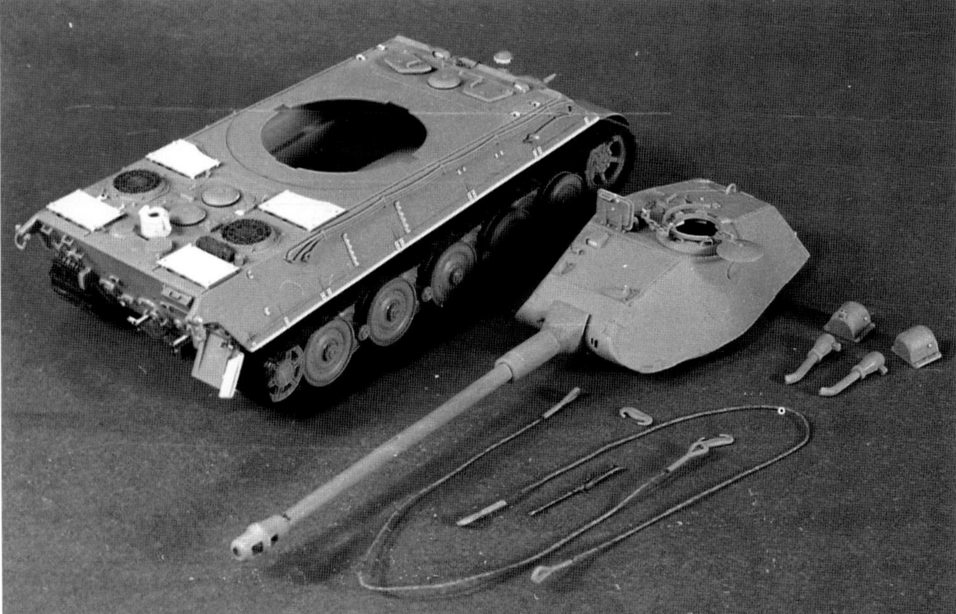

The model is ready for painting. This overall view clearly shows off the added detail in white plasticard. The track mounting cables on the sponson sides can be fixed before painting without any problem. They do not interfere with the weathering procedures later on.

There is not much to say about the Nichimo kit. It is basically the same as the kit with the Henschel turret and moreover, it is the only available model with a Porsche turret, so you have to settle for it. In general, detailing is the same as the kit we discussed on page 16 and on and the following pictures tell the whole story. The diorama is not too special either except for the Raupenschlepper Ost from Italeri. So, why not tell a little about the Tiger units.

The Tigers (Es and Bs) where organized in Heavy Battalions. The Army formed eleven of them numbered 501 through 511 plus one training battalion n°500. The SS later on had three independent battalions 101 to 103. Each Panzer Division was supposed to get its own heavy battalion.

In theory a Heavy Battalion was comprised of a battalion headquarters with three Tigers, and four companies with two company HQ tanks plus three four-tank platoons. Thus a heavy Battalion would total 59 Tigers. But, as said, this was only theory. In practice, battalions having enough heavies to form three organic companies were very lucky. Many units had to settle for two companies of Tigers and a number of PzKpfw IIINs to complement them.

Designation of the units was as follows : sPzAbt 2/501 meant schwere Panzer Abteilung (heavy armor unit), 2 Kompanie (2nd company), 501 Battalion.

The tank registration number 231 denoted n°2 company, n°3 platoon, n°1 tank. Some Heavy Battalions adopted the name of the division they supported, for instance sPzAbt 'GD' stood for 'schwere Panzer Abteilung Gross Deutschland' or 13/SS-PRI LLSAH meant '13 company/SS Panzer Regiment I Leibstandarte Adolf Hitler'.
Besides these battalions various units of Tiger variants were formed. The fates of all these units have been elaborately described in many books of excellent quality.

Although the Tiger was a legendary fighting machine it lacked speed, range and agility. It was therefor best in the defending role. However, it came too late to play a decisive part in the course of the war. The Heavy Units won many local battles but did not change the final outcome of WWII. One question stays open : 'Would they ever have been able to do so?'

The brass grenades and empty shell cases were made on a lathe. The wooden crates had to be scratchbuilt. Should you want to do the same, the dimensions and shapes are noted on the next page.

To get the ditch right you have to use styrofoam to elevate the surrounding ground. Final shaping was done with a modeling paste. When the static grass has been added the tracks have to be pressed in the still soft paste. 68 tons leave their marks. The small bridge was sculpted with epoxy putty on a piece of wood. The water in the ditch was painted on the base plate.

No supply stop is complete without a load of fuel for the gas hungry Tigers.

An overall view of the finished Tiger on the diorama clearly shows the importance of tuning the weathering of a vehicle to the surrounding area. Washing and drybrushing into the blue without knowing what your diorama will look like leaves you with a lot of trouble in the end.
The figures featured on this diorama have again been composed from various parts out of the scrapbox.

The old Peerless kit of the Steyr Raupenschlepper Ost is now marketed by Italeri. The model is an excellent secondary vehicle on the diorama.

8.8 cm Ammunition In Detail

8.8 cm KwK 43 Anti-tank

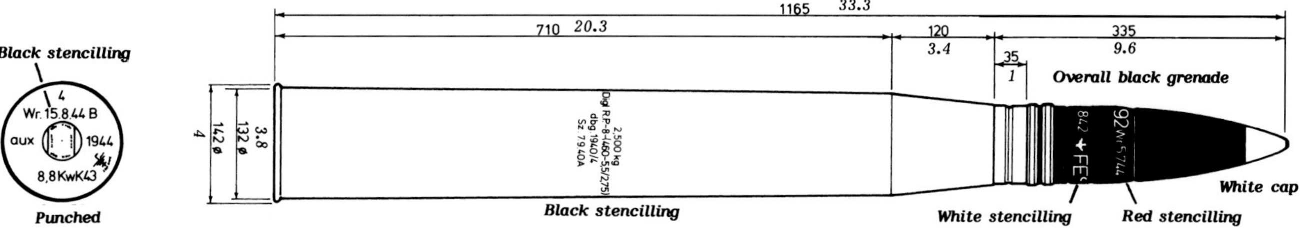

8.8 cm Flak 46 High Explosive

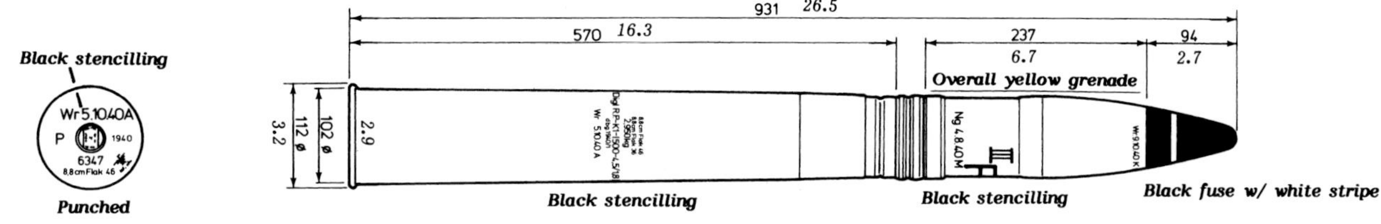

8.8 cm Flak 18 Anti-tank

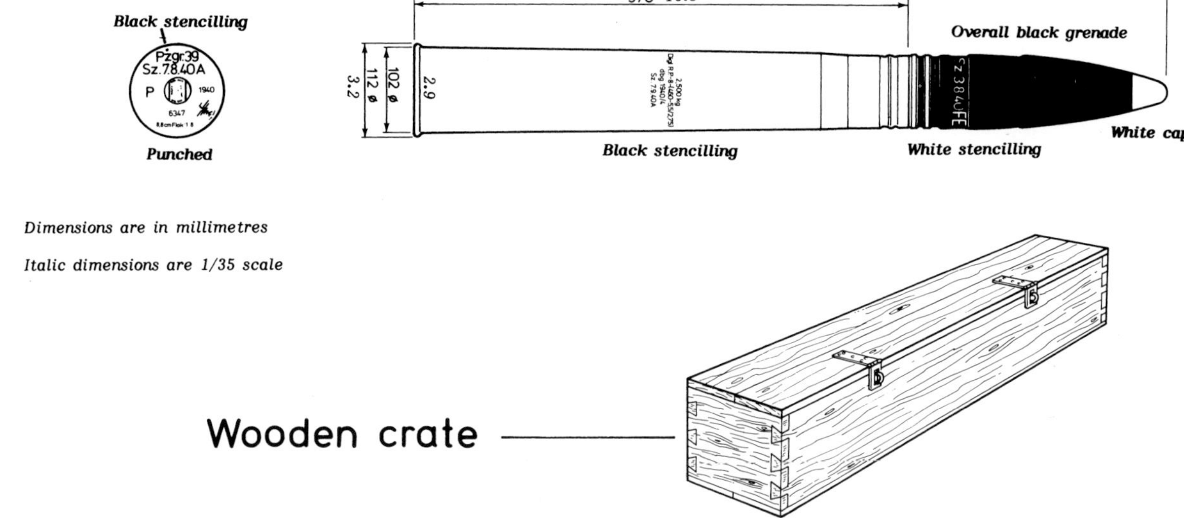

Dimensions are in millimetres

Italic dimensions are 1/35 scale

Wooden crate

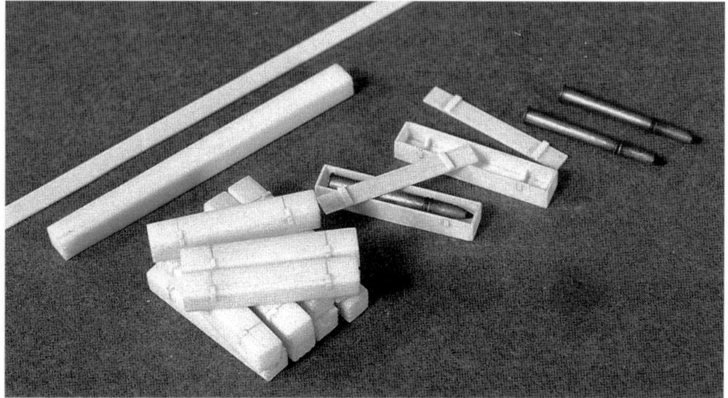

Panzerjäger TIGER (P) 'Elefant' SdKfz 184

Specifications

Total weight	65,000 kg
Power plant	2 x Maybach HL120 TRM V12 12 Liter 265 PK
Armament	Stuk 43/1 L/71 88mm
	1 MG 34 (loose)
Ammunition	55 rounds 88 mm
	600 rounds 7.92 mm
Top speed	20 km/h
Crew	6

Booby Trap !

The tank killer Tiger (Porsche) Ferdinand, later nicknamed 'Elefant', was one of the least succesful sub-versions of the entire Tiger family. The vehicle was based on the hull of the Porsche 'Königstiger'. When the Henschel and Porsche Königstiger were still prototypes Porsche was awarded a contract for a number of vehicles. As we have already seen, the Henschel design proved to be superior; the Porsche turrets were sent to Henschel and the former was stuck with a lot of finished hulls.

Although it was pointed out to him that trials were still unsatisfactory, Hitler insisted on immediately equipping the hulls with a superstructure mounting a 8.8cm PaK43 and pressing them into service.

The Elefant first saw action during operation 'Zitadelle' at Kursk in July 1943. The two units at battalion strength blew large breaches in the Soviet defense only to be closed in by the surviving troops from the sides and the rear, and were destroyed with grenades, Molotov cocktails and mines.

The lack of close-in defensive armament forced the crew to shoot individuals with the main gun. Approaching an Elefant unseen from the sides or the rear was a piece of cake. During home land overhaul the remaining Ferdinands received a machinegun at the radio-operator's position, a commander's cupola and an additional gun mantlet. A number of vehicles were sent to Italy, but the constant trouble with the gasoline-electric drive caused too much trouble for the Elefant to be really effective. Many vehicles were abandoned as no repair facilities were at hand.

The Italeri kit is basically a very good model and only requires a little extra-detailling. Here drains for rain water have been added. Barely visible is the gunner's periscope sight peeping trough a hatch on the roof.

The job of applying zimmerit is done. This picture shows the result before painting and weathering. You will find a complete zimmerit story elsewhere in this book.

The fenders and fender and headlight mounts can do with a little additional detail as well.

Another detail view of the Zimmerit, this time the front of the vehicle. Note the periscopes in front of the driver's hatch made from very heavy plasticard.

This picture clearly shows the result of the painted and weathered model. The effect of the pyrograph-applied zimmerit is very realistic. The logo on both superstructure sides was handpainted. The registration number denoting n°1 company HQ, vehicle n°2 was made up with dry transfers readily available from any stationery shop.

At left : An overall rear view again illustrates the natural appearance of the finished model. As you may have noticed, this Elefant is of the late type as is witnessed by the commander's copula, the bolted-on gun mantlet and the ball mounted machinegun.

With this total view of the finished scene we start a series of pictures showing you the idea behind the diorama. The MDA ruin was specially designed for this scene, but is available in our range of bunkers and ruins. Just ask your local dealer.

The remnants of the second floor made from balsa beams and planking.

Small details on a diorama add a lot to the life-like appearance. The wine bottle on the window sill is one of those details.

These pictures show some more of the details we were talking about.
The well comes with the MDA kit but should be detailed. The iron frame and the pully block are homemade as well as the remnants of the iron fences. The shutter on the bottom left picture was made from plasticard. The drain pipe is simply a piece

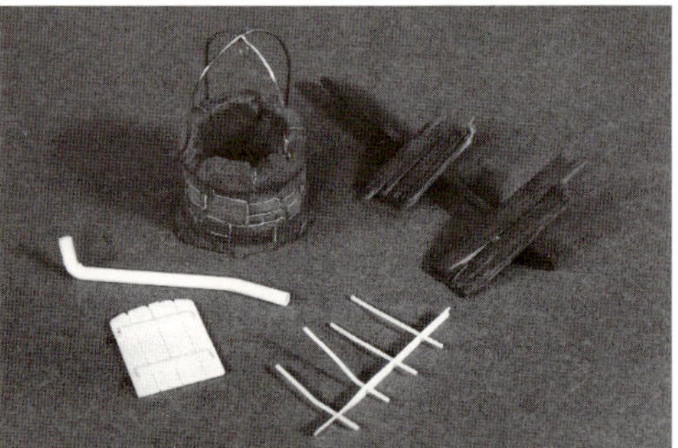

of plastic rod. It can easily be bent by carefully warming the material over a candle flame or even better a light bulb of some 75 watts.

The pictures on this page speak for themselves. The best way to learn the tricks of the trade is to carefully study these photos. Pay attention to the subtle shading of the colors, the arrangement of the debris and the various realistic details.

Elefant Details

This detail shot offers a good view on the engine louvres, hull hatches and back of the additional gun mantlet.

Note on this picture how the applique armour was bolted and welded to the hull.

The front of the additional gun mantlet on the final production type 'Elefant'.

Track, sprocket and road wheel detail as well as a good view of the skirt attachment.

The loader's hatch in detail. Note the small hinged section which could be used for an extra periscope.

The ball mount for an MG was added after the bad experiences in Russia. The rough weld job is very obvious in this picture.

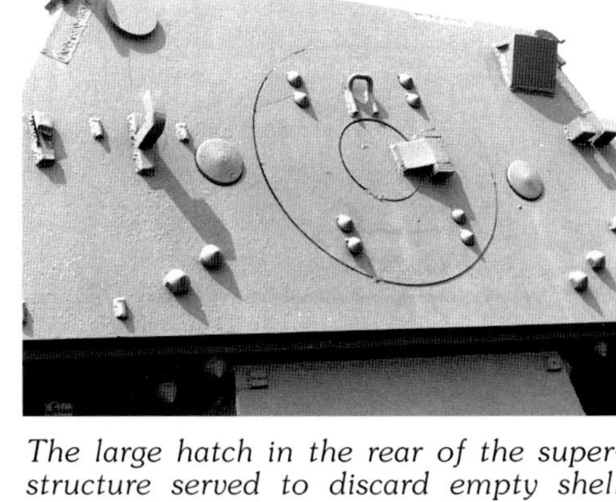

The large hatch in the rear of the superstructure served to discard empty shell cases, remove the gun, and as an escape hatch.

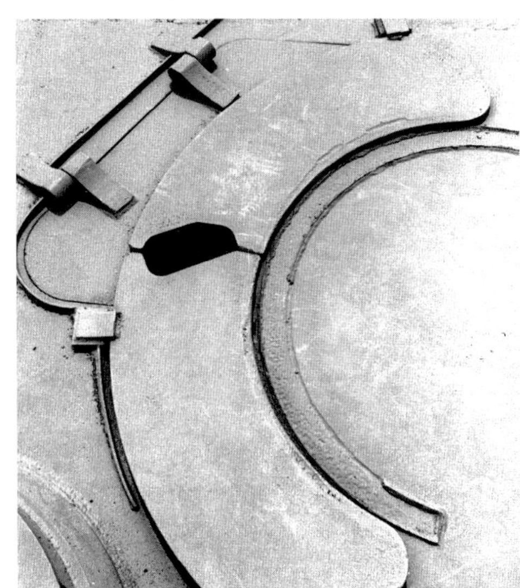

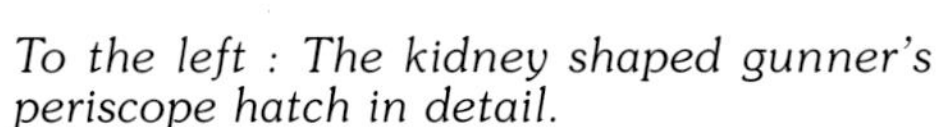

Another shot of the bolted-on mantlet. Note the attachment of the superstructure to the hull.

To the left : The kidney shaped gunner's periscope hatch in detail.

This picture reveals that the armored cover of the exhaust mufflers is slightly different from the one on the kit. The toolbox is missing here.

Battle Damage

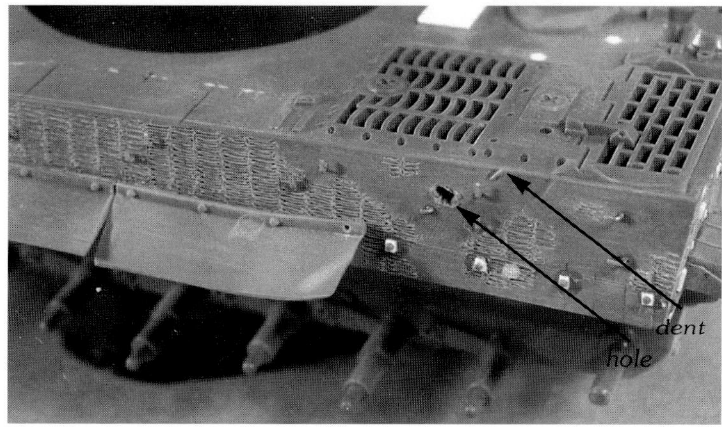

The hole in the hull side in the center of this picture was made with the pyrograph set at moderate heat. Push it through the plastic and jerk it around to shape the edges of the hole. To the top right of the hole, on the edge of the side plate, is a dent caused by a bouncing shell. You can make this with a file.

This is why the Tiger was the Allied tanker's nightmare. Three consecutive hits from a 76mm anti-tank gun merely resulted in three nice dents and a somewhat dazzled crew. This picture clearly shows the effect of a shaped charge on heavy armour.

The effect of small arms fire, probably a machine gun, on the sloping side armour of the Königstiger. These dents can be made with a ball shaped dentist's drill bit.

Concentrated small arms fire resulted in dents in the turret armor and big hunks of zimmerit coming off.

Zimmerit

A very basic feature of late war German tanks was the so-called zimmerit. Real book worms can probably tell you the chemical composition of the stuff, but basically it is a special, extra thick cement. The Germans, like everybody else, were very concerned with the devastating effect of magnetic mines stuck to their precious tanks by daredevil infantry, especially on the Eastern front.

They were the only ones to come up with an effective solution: zimmerit. This paste, applied in a certain minimum thickness, prevented magnetic mines from sticking to the armor steel. It was factory-applied to all armored vehicles powerful enough to carry the extra weight around.

Zimmerit being a specific feature on German armor, many modelers may want to go about it. First of all you can use putty and apply it with a toothed blade. Whatever putty you use, plastic filler or an epoxy type, it is a very messy operation and you can easily louse it up. It is very difficult to blank off the areas that have to remain clean and you end up with a little putty on the model and a lot everywhere else. It is pretty tough not to lose your patience. There is an easier, cleaner and probably more effective way. Of course, you need to buy a pyrograph, but it is not a bad investment. It can be used for many other purposes like simulating battle damage, welding plastic parts or even marking your model with a signature. How do you simulate zimmerit with a pyrograph?

First you finish constructing your model, but without fixing small parts, like hooks and brackets, and bigger parts that might interfere with the job, like track skirts, exhaust mufflers, and so on.

Left : This is what actual, aged Zimmerit looks like. Note the thickness of the layer and that it has been applied in bands about 3" wide.

You should not forget to mark their position in pencil. Then you have to decide where the zimmerit is to go or not. Clean areas should be outlined as well. Next you divide the Zimmerit areas up into equal, vertical bands of about 3 to 4mm (3/16") wide. Then you can take the pyrograph and carefully draw horizontal lines in the platic. As there are many kinds of plastic, soft and hard, you should check the heat of the tip on a piece of scrap. The plastic should not melt too easily, so start at moderate heat.

When you have finished all zimmerit areas you might have to clean up some burrs and you are all set to finish the model.

The 'bands' of zimmerit have been indicated on the model in plastic. Note that certain areas, where no zimmerit is to be applied, have been outlined as well.

Before you start 'pyrographing' into the blue you should carefully plan the when and where. Zimmerit was not applied to parts that had to bve removed every once and a while, like the dome covers of the track tension draw-bolts, etc. Also note that the areas where the exhaust mufflers and their covers are mounted are left free of zimmerit.

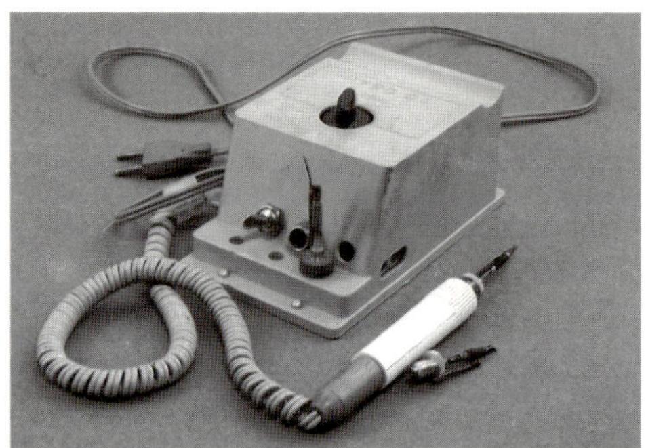

The pyrograph can be a modeler's best friend when used properly. It will make it easy on you to simulate battle damage and zimmerit.

This is what your model should look like when you have finished simulating zimmerit using the pyrograph. Before you tackle the model you should practice on scrap.

In the picture below we see the realistic effect of zimmerit applied with the pyrograph on a burned out hulk. Like with every detail on plastic models a good dry-brush job is the finishing touch. A little practice won't hurt. Also pay some attention to the battle damage.

Since the original release of this book (1984) a lot of kits have been released and even discontinued. On this page you will find updates for Tiger kits that are active Verlinden Products as of January 1998.

VP 406 Tiger II Engine Type B&E Maybach HP230P45 1/35 scale

VP 431 Tiger I Engine Maybach HP230P30 1/35 scale

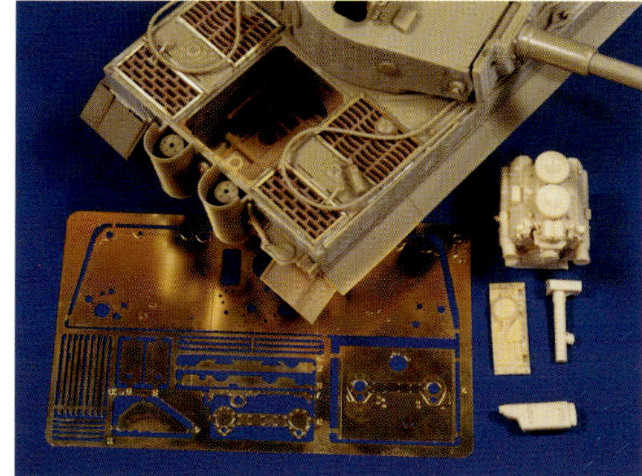

VP 526 Tiger I Engine Compartment 1/35 scale

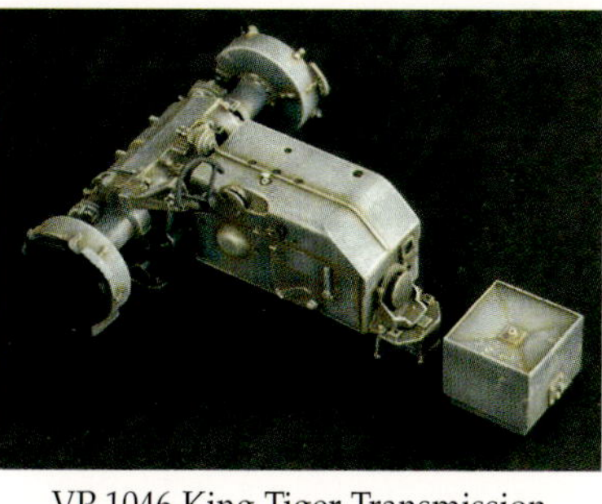

VP 1046 King Tiger Transmission 1/35 scale

VP 1049 Tiger I Transmission 1/35 scale

VP 1045 King Tiger Engine Compartment (for Tamiya) 1/35 scale

VP 1177 Tiger I Detail Set 1/35 scale

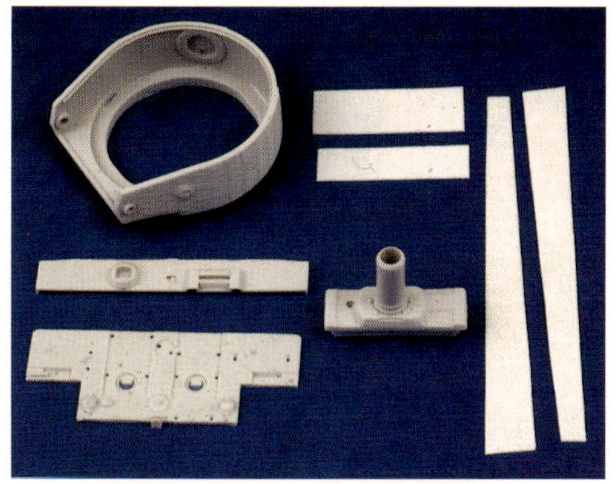

VP 1250 Zimmerit for Tiger IE 1/35 scale

VP 863 Tiger I Ausf.E 1 1/15 scale

VP 1019 Tiger I Engine & Compartment 1/15 scale

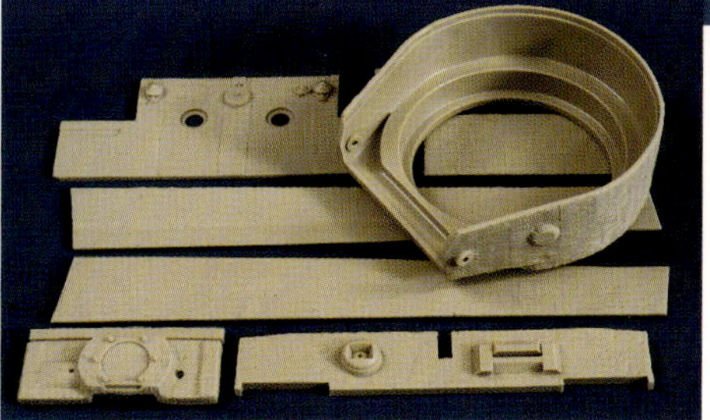

VP 864 Zimmerit Kit for Tiger I 1/15 scale

VERLINDEN PUBLICATIONS
WARMACHINES SERIES

THE ULTIMATE REFERENCE FOR
THE ARMOR MODELER AND ENTHUSIAST

N°0496 WARMACHINES N°1
M108-M109-M109 A1/A2

N°0505 WARMACHINES N°2
M113 A1/A2 - M577 A1/A2

N°0542 WARMACHINES N°3
M60 A3

N°0555 WARMACHINES N°4
ISRAELI M4 SHERMAN

N°0580 WARMACHINES N°5
BRADLEY M2/M3

N°0581 WARMACHINES N°6
M1 ABRAMS

N°0600 WARMACHINES N°7
M998 HMMWV HUMMER

N°0626 WARMACHINES N°8
A GULF WAR EYEWITNESS REPORT

N°0668 WARMACHINES N°9
M113/PART 2

N°0669 WARMACHINES N°10
IDF T-54/T-55/T-62 MINI

N°0694 WARMACHINES N°11
MERKAVA MK2/MK3 MINI

N°0695 WARMACHINES N°12
MLRS

N°0735 WARMACHINES N°13
"On the Road to Kuwait"

N°0760 WARMACHINES N°14
M151 "MUTT" MINI

N°0857 WARMACHINES N°15
3/325 ABCT BLUE FALCONS

N°0929 WARMACHINES N°16
GERMAN INFANTRY IN ACTION

N°0736 WARMACHINES PLUS
VOL.I - WILLYS, DODGE, GMCs

N°0858 ARMOR IN DETAIL
TIGER I

N°0939 ARMOR IN DETAIL
PANTHER AUSF.A